PROPERTIES of MATERIALS

WILL IT FLOAT OR SINK?

BY LISA J. AMSTUTZ

PEBBLE
a capstone imprint

Pebble Emerge is published by Pebble, an imprint of Capstone.
1710 Roe Crest Drive North Mankato, Minnesota 56003
www.capstonepub.com

Library of Congress Cataloging-in-Publication Data is availble on the Library of Congress website.
ISBN: 978-1-9771-3177-5 (hardcover)
ISBN: 978-1-9771-3284-0 (paperback)
ISBN: 978-1-9771-5539-9 (eBook PDF)

Summary: A rubber duck floats in the tub. A rock sinks to the bottom of a lake. Why do some objects float and others sink?

Image Credits
Shutterstock: Alexander Hoffmann, 16, Alexapicso, Cover, 8, Avigator Fortuner, 12, Cozine, middle left 9, Hayati Kayhan, 5, Ilya Andriyanov, 20, Mariyana M, 17, Mirage_studio, 11, Monkey Business Images, 7, oksana2010, 4, Pat_Hastings, middle left 19, middle right 19, SeDmi, 13, Thitisan, middle right 9, tkemot, 14, Valentin Valkov, 15, vectorplus, (comic) design element throughout

Editorial Credits
Editor: Michelle Parkin; Designer: Sarah Bennett; Media Researcher: Morgan Walters; Production Specialist: Laura Manthe

All internet sites appearing in back matter were available and accurate when this book was sent to press.

Printed and bound in China. PO4205

Table of Contents

Words in **bold** are in the glossary.

Will It Float?

The next time you take a bath, drop your soap in the tub. What happens? It sinks to the bottom. Now drop a rubber duck into the tub. It floats to the top. But why?

The soap and rubber duck are made of different **materials**. They have different **properties**. They do not act the same way in water.

Matter Matters

Everything around you is made of **matter**. The soap and rubber duck are made of matter. So is the water in the tub.

Matter is made up of tiny particles called **atoms**. In some objects, the atoms are tightly packed together. In other objects, the atoms are spread out. The amount of matter in a space is called **density**.

More Dense, Less Dense

There are three types of matter—solids, liquids, and gases. A bowling ball is a solid object. The atoms of matter are close together.

Water is a liquid. The atoms are more spread apart.

Air is a gas. The atoms of matter in a gas are spread even farther apart.

How can you tell if an object will float or sink in water? It depends on the object's density.

Put a bowling ball in the water. The solid ball is denser than the water. It sinks to the bottom.

What about a balloon? There is air inside the balloon. Air is less dense than water. The balloon floats on top.

A ship weighs a lot. How can it float? A ship holds lots of air inside. The air makes the ship less dense than the water. It floats.

Let's see how this works. A boat made out of foil floats in water. If you put coins inside, it still floats.

If the foil boat is crushed into a ball, however, it will sink. It still weighs the same amount. But the ball is more dense than the boat.

Upward Forces

Liquids like water push items up. This is called **buoyancy**.

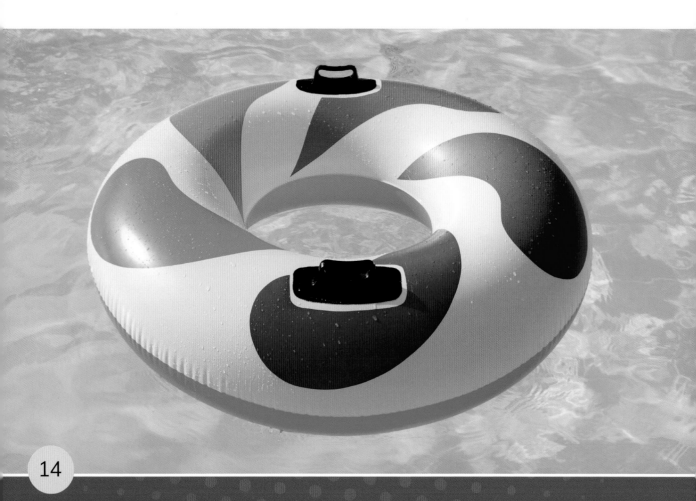

An object's shape affects buoyancy.
A boat is wider than a bowling ball. There
is more water to push the boat up.

You can change the density of water. Just add salt. Let's see how this works. Put a grape in a cup of water. The grape sinks to the bottom. The grape is denser than the water.

Now add salt to the water and stir. The grape floats this time. The grape is not as dense as the salty water.

Do Liquids Float?

Can a liquid float in another liquid? Let's find out. Take oil and water. These liquids have different densities. Oil is less dense than water. That means oil will float on the water's surface.

Look around your home. What can you find that will float? What can you find that will sink?

Sinking Scavenger Hunt

Test different objects around your home to see if they sink or float.

What You Need:

- small bucket filled with water

- plastic cup

- metal spoon

- craft stick

- rock (about as big as your fist)

- apple

- leaf

What You Do:

1. Draw a line down the middle of a piece of paper. On the left side, write "sink." On the right side, write "float."

2. Take a close look at each object. Pick it up and hold it in your hand. Do you think it will sink or float in water? Write your guess on the paper.

3. Put the plastic cup into the water. Watch what happens. Did you guess correctly?

4. Repeat the test with the other items. Circle the items you guessed correctly on your chart.

Glossary

atom (AT-uhm)—the smallest part of matter

buoyancy (BOO-yen-see)—the ability to float in water or air

density (DEN-sih-tee)—the amount of matter in an area

material (muh-TEER-ee-ul)—the stuff a thing is made of

matter (MAT-ter)—anything that has weight and takes up space

property (PROP-ur-tee)—a quality of a material, such as color, hardness, or shape

Read More

Peterson, Megan Cooley. *Matter.* North Mankato, MN: Pebble, a Capstone imprint, 2020.

Williams, Rozanne. *What Sinks? What Floats?* Cypress, CA: Creative Teaching Press, 2017.

Zalewski, Aubrey. *Sink vs. Float.* Mankato, MN: The Child's World, 2020.

Internet Sites

All About Sink and Float
easyscienceforkids.com/all-about-sink-and-float/

Float or Sink?
ideastream.pbslearningmedia.org/resource/ket-earlychild-sci10/sink-or-float

Sink or Float?
sciencenetlinks.com/lessons/sink-or-float/

Index